Contents

The routes described in this book have been abbreviated to cut out unnecessary words and keep the text as concise as possible.
The description of a route or track is not evidence of a right of way.
Any compass bearings stated are given as magnetic bearings.

It is recommended that a compass and the following maps are used in conjunction with these walks: -
Ordnance Survey Explorer No. 270 Sherwood Forest
Ordnance Survey Explorer No. 271 Newark
Ordnance Survey Explorer No. 279 Doncaster

PF = Public Footpath
PB = Public Bridleway
CP = Car Park

Walk 1: Carlton Wood Walk
Walk Time: 1hr 25mins   Distance: 5.5km   3.4miles
Start / Park: GR 588839 Map No. 279

1. Park beside St. John the Evangelist Church in South Carlton. Go through opening in stonewall next to telegraph pole opposite church.
2. Go through small 5-bar gate then cross diagonally over field to wooden 5-bar gate at far side.
3. Pass tennis court on left following hedge and path anti-clockwise to Carlton Wood.
4. Walk on main path through wood for 160m then turn right at a crossroads in path (beside large fir tree) onto a narrower path leading to rear of houses at Carlton in Lindrick.
5. On reaching rear of houses turn left to walk to far end.
6. At end of houses turn right, look for **PF** sign on left leading up to farm and passing riding stables on right. Pass between farm buildings then cross stile onto farm lane. Cross lane to **PF** at far side.
7. Continue on narrow path with woodland on left and fields to right. Cross another track then 400m further is a distinct 'S' bend in the track. Just past this turn left passing between two stone pillars at each side of track.
8. Continue to sign pointing in 4 directions then walk straight ahead for 200m through a narrow strip of woodland then over a small bridge to a lane.
9. You emerge on a bend on a lane. Bear right to ascend to a **PF** sign at top. Turn left at top towards Holme House Farm, passing a row of bungalows.
10. Just past farm entrance go through an opening in fence following yellow arrow along by hedge. Do not go into next field but follow hedge towards house called Owday Lodge, which you should see ahead.
11. Turn left past front of house, then left again on **PF** bearing 527°M from sign at far side of house towards farm (large house) across fields. Look for a church and path bears to right of it.
12. Beside large house follow path to road and back to church where you started.

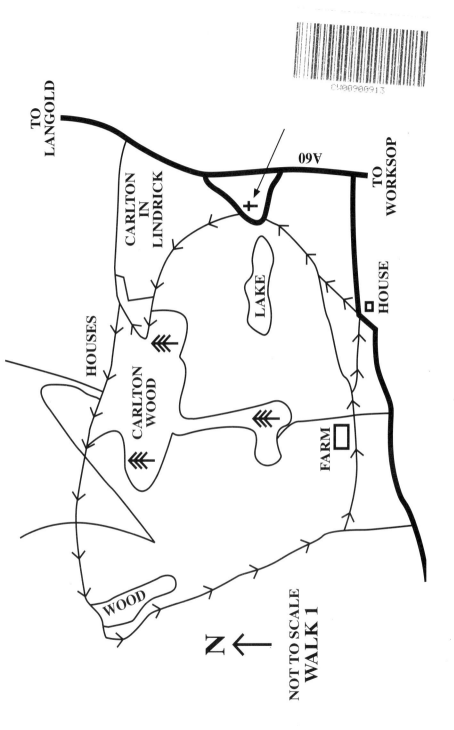

TO LANGOLD

TO WORKSOP

A60

CARLTON IN LINDRICK

HOUSES

CARLTON WOOD

LAKE

HOUSE

FARM

WOOD

N

NOT TO SCALE
WALK 1

Walk 2: Langold / Nature Reserve Walk
Walk Time: 1hr 45mins   Distance: 6.2km   3.9miles
Start / Park: GR 564886 Map No. 279

1. Park in parking area opposite The Black Lion pub in Firbeck. Look for **PB** sign pointing past Parkhill social club.
2. Follow track descending by houses then woodland on left before ascending Salt Hill to the B6463 at Salt Hill Lodge GR 570881.
3. Cross road taking **PB** on left through woods then alongside hedge on distinct track to Dyscarr Wood.
4. Just as you reach the left corner of Dyscarr Wood follow path ahead looking for sign on right into Dyscarr Wood Nature Reserve.
5. Follow path due south through wood, pass a football field then bear left by school and houses. Keep on main track to south end of wood.
6. At end of wood turn right on **PB** through wood then passing open fields before joining Ivy Lodge Lane at GR 568871.
7. At right-hand bend in lane go straight ahead towards Letwell for 300m. Approaching first houses turn right on a track keeping hedge to your left.
8. Emerge on B6463 on Lamb Lane. Cross with care, follow PF sign ascending over open field bearing 359°M from **PF** sign. Cross diagonally over farm access road on same bearing to the right of Firbeck Church to emerge on Kid Lane. Turn left up to church.
9. At main road by church turn right 230m back to parking area near The Black Lion pub.

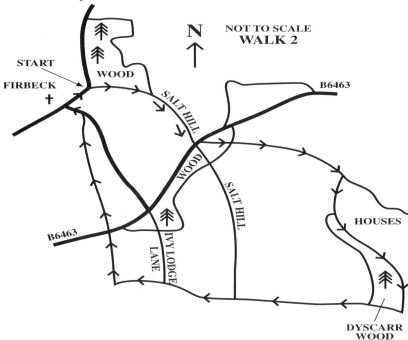

4

Walk 3: River Trent Walk (Near Sturton Le Steeple)
Walk Time: 2hrs   Distance: 7km   4.3miles
Start / Park: GR 801844 Map No. 271

1. Park at end of Common Lane where you meet **PB**. Turn right along Cross Common Lane (wide stony lane) for 700m.
2. At crossroads turn left onto Upper Ings Lane walking for 1.7km to a wide drain dyke with a 4-way **PB** sign. This is Middle Lane / South End Lane.
3. Continue in same direction towards River Trent. On reaching river go through 5-bar gate to ascend flood defence banking then bear left following the course of the river.
4. You can either walk around the first bend in the river or carry straight on along the banking.
5. Just past the next sharp bend in river you come to a drain ditch on your left. Turn left here along North End Lane. Walk for 1.1km to first lane on right called Cow pasture Lane.
6. Stay on this for 1.7km passing a lane on right followed by a short bend in lane.
7. At a left-hand bend in lane you pass another lane on right. Stay on main lane, which should take you back to where you parked your vehicle.

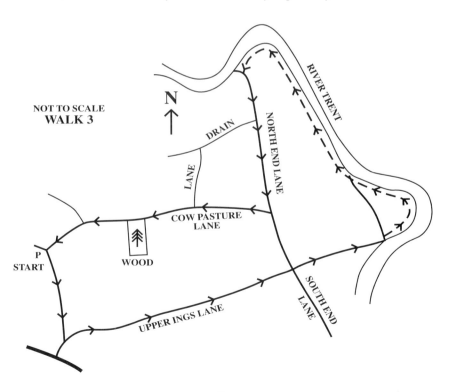

Walk 4: Laneham Walk
Walk Time: 1hr 50min   **Distance: 7.2km 4.5miles**
Start / Park: GR 809747   Map No. 271

1. Start and park beside a sign stating Chequers Lane. Walk up here **(PF)** past houses and sign 'private road Manor Farm only'. Pass a white house on your left, walk straight ahead to the last house looking for **PF** sign beside 5-bar gate. Cross stile following main track (not **PF** sign on right) diagonally across field.
2. Track winds round to another 5-bar gate. Cross stile next to gate onto narrow grass path at side of field with a dyke on right.
3. Go through small gate at far side then over small wooden bridge. Walk ahead on grass track between 2 fields towards Church Laneham. Stay on track to near Manor Farm then bear left to minor road.
4. Cross road to **PF** sign then into field walking round left side of house to far right side of field. Look for opening into next field.
5. Now walk at rear of houses bearing left on a raised grass track. You see a church on right then cross 2 stiles and concrete bridge followed by 2 kissing gates into field alongside caravan site.
6. Walk to right of house at entrance to Manor House Caravan Park then onto minor road by the river. Turn left staying on minor road for 150m.
7. Approaching houses on right, turn left on **PF** (Maltkilns) along side of caravan park 200m further. At end of track take **PF** sign to right looking for small posts in field denoting diagonal path bearing 306°M from the **PF** sign.
8. Walk for 250m then join another **PF** where you turn right walking nearby parallel with overhead power lines over field to the minor road (Helenship Lane). At the road turn left for 800m to Broading Farm on corner.
9. Turn left again along Broadings Lane, a wide stony track for 1.2km to junction at minor road in Laneham. At minor road cross onto **PF** by side of farm. Cross 2 stiles then over small bridge. Turn right for 150m to Trent Valley Way on left.
10. Stay on the Trent Valley Way, which leads onto Chequers Lane. Go over stile and along by narrow dyke under power lines. Continue straight ahead now on a wide track. At farm buildings cross stile ahead to walk along by hedge.
11 Cross next stile looking for **PF** you started on. Turn right back to start point on Chequers Lane.

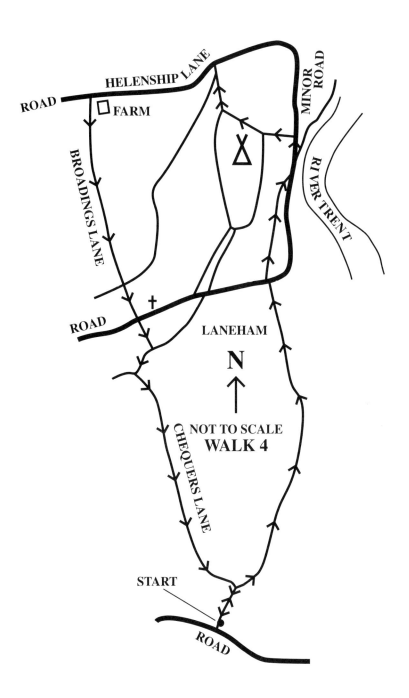

ROAD

HELENSHIP LANE

☐ FARM

MINOR ROAD

BROADINGS LANE

RIVER TRENT

ROAD

†

LANEHAM

N
↑

NOT TO SCALE
WALK 4

CHEQUERS LANE

START

ROAD

Walk 5: Hodsock Priory Walk
Walk Time: 2hrs 20min   Distance: 13.4km   5.4miles
Start: GR 593846 Map No. 279

1. Park on side road in Carlton in Lindrick. **PF** off main road called Greenway. Look for narrow path between houses & **PF** sign.
2. Walk on path along back of houses then cross several stiles alongside hedge and side of fields. Keep in same direction for 2.1km to the priory.
3. Arriving at junction near Priory, look for dove house on left in garden. Turn left at junction following lane.
4. A triangle of grass is at side of road in front of priory archway entrance, look for 5-bar gate on left with small blue arrow on it, as you go round the slight bend.
5. Go through, walking diagonally across field, bearing 10°M from gate towards small group of pine trees at far side on the higher ground.
6. Pass the right side of the trees; look for stile a short distance away. Cross to walk across field bearing 35°M from stile towards Winks Wood.
7. Walk through Winks Wood to a minor road then turn left continuing on road to Hodsock Cottage.
8. Keep on this potholed track to walk anti clockwise to Hodsock Lodge Farm GR 600864 ahead. Approaching the farm go to left of buildings by an open barn, walking towards the farmhouse.
9. Turn left on track by a hedge, walk towards Horse Pasture Wood ahead. 250m before wood another hedge leads off to the right. Walk on this track now towards North Carlton.
10. You eventually join a narrow road; walk on this for 180m to meet another road on left. Turn left then immediately right onto a **PF** at side of house with a football field on right.
11. Go over stile to rejoin path you started on. Turn right back to start.

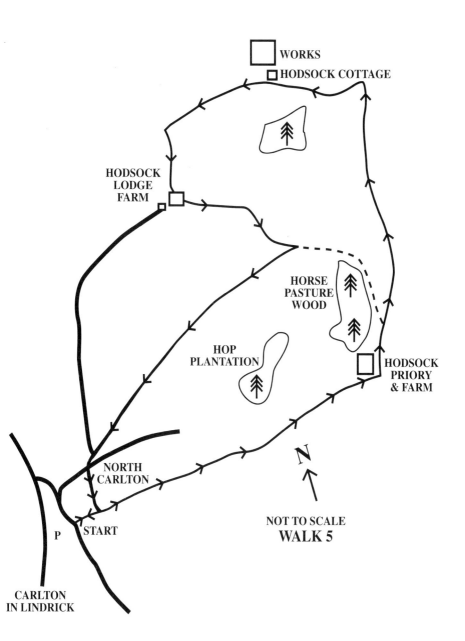

WORKS

HODSOCK COTTAGE

HODSOCK
LODGE
FARM

HORSE
PASTURE
WOOD

HOP
PLANTATION

HODSOCK
PRIORY
& FARM

N

NORTH
CARLTON

NOT TO SCALE
WALK 5

P   START

CARLTON
IN LINDRICK

9

Walk 6: Clumber Park Walk
Walk Time: 2hrs 40mins   Distance: 9.4km   5.8 miles
Start: GR 611762 Map No. 270

1. Start at **CP** 700m from Truman's Lodge, Clumber Park.
2. Turn left on minor road for 500m to **PB** on right into woods.
3. Walk 1.1km in a straight line to Limetree Avenue (trees on both sides)
4. Turn left for 50m then right bearing 115°M from road walking on path by side of trees.
5. Just before narrow road turn left at blue **PF** sign through wood. At road cross diagonally on PF through wood.
6. At next road turn right for 450m to just before Hardwick Village. Turn right again down a road to Clumber Lake.
7. Walk past 1st part of lake then bear left on an obvious path near some short posts. Ascend through Ash Tree Hill Wood to a wider track crossing your path.
8. Turn left then right 40m further, on a narrow path leading to a pair of 5-bar gates and an open field beyond.
9. Look ahead for church spire, GR 627746, taking path across field towards it. Cross stile then pass a cycle hire and houses.
10. Pass **CP** at right-hand bend in road turn left towards lake. Keep right on path near lake, pass pine trees on your right.
11. At barrier and small **CP** on left, take narrow path on left towards lake again and a small island. Look for a weir and small stone building on left.
12. You come to an arched bridge (Clumber Bridge) turn right 150m to junction (do not cross bridge). Turn left at road junction.
13. Walk for 580m to a barrier across road with small hut next to it. Continue ahead to Limetree Avenue. Cross this road looking for track to Carburton Hills.
14. Walk generally in a north easterly direction on a track through woodland for 2.8km to Truman's Lodge (gatehouse). At the lodge a road turns right back to the **CP** 700m further.

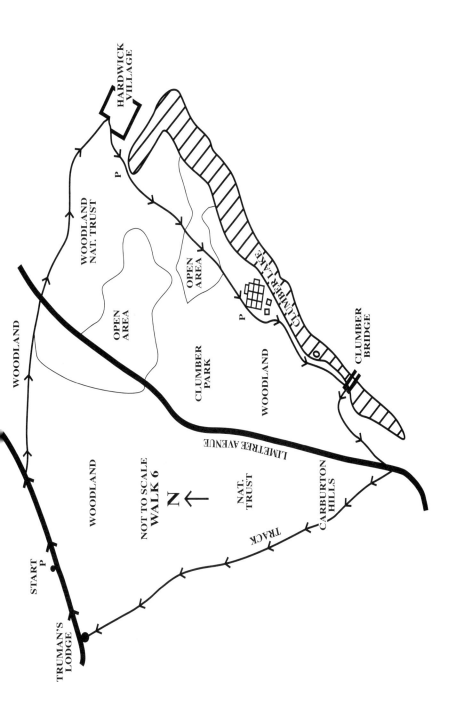

HARDWICK VILLAGE

WOODLAND NAT. TRUST

P

OPEN AREA

WOODLAND

OPEN AREA

CLUMBER PARK

CLUMBER LAKE

P

WOODLAND

CLUMBER BRIDGE

LIMETREE AVENUE

WOODLAND

NOT TO SCALE
WALK 6

N

NAT. TRUST

CARBURTON HILLS

TRACK

START
P

TRUMAN'S LODGE

Walk 7: Headon Walk
Walk Time: 3hrs 15mins   Distance: 11.5km 7.2miles
Start: GR 751770 Map No. 271

This walk is more challenging and may require use of map/compass skills to navigate over open fields.

1. Park on corner of Thorpe St. and bridleway entrance to farm buildings. Leave access for vehicles.

2. Walk southeast on bridleway for 500m looking for first **PF** on left over stile. Cross field bearing 38°M. At stile on far side continue to road.

3. At road cross then follow bearing 43°M to corner of field, crossing farm track. Continue same direction over 2 fields looking for opening in hedge, turn right for 50m then left across field by hedge. Turn right 30m then bear left walking diagonally right to road. Look for openings in fields.

4. At road turn left for 500m to Bottom Woodbeck Farm GR 760782. Look for **PF** in far corner of bend, cross field to far left corner of small wood. Take general bearing 26°M to corner of Treswell Wood GR 760790. Take care here not to go into small sections of woodland on left.

5. At left corner of Treswell Wood follow path/track round left side of woodland for 1.2km to road. Turn left. Walking for 500m to Grove Manor Farm.

6. Opposite farm take **PF** on left bearing 213°M for 50m then bear 288°M to right of field. From opening in hedge take general bearing of 264°M to take you over 3 fields to a bend in the road. Turn left on road then right at **PF** sign bearing 289°M ascending left of a TV/radio mast.

7. Emerge onto track, cross it then walk by side of hedge GR 741802 in same direction to a stile. Walk along the left side of Castle Hill Wood and over open area in same direction to near corner of next wood. At stile turn left bearing 160°M across 2 fields then joining another path leading to the minor road through Grove.

8. Emerging beside the post box, cross road onto **PF** at far side for 50m then bear right bearing 172°M from **PF** sign for 500m over 2 fields before turning left on general bearing 142°M crossing a further 2 fields.

9. At opening in hedge bear 120°M to far side of field then 162°M to right of Ladywell Rise (collection of buildings). Where path divides take left fork to take you to the road at side of Ladywell Rise GR 750780.

10. At the busy road cross with care following path over 2 fields towards the church you should see in Headon. Follow the **PF** by the houses back to your starting point in Headon.

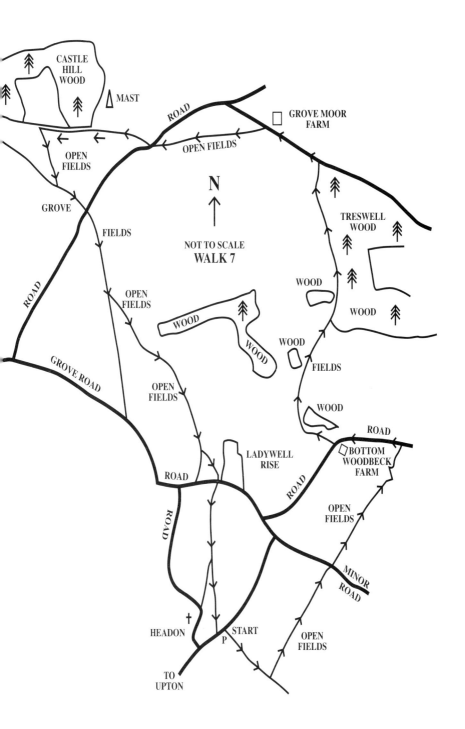

CASTLE
HILL
WOOD

△ MAST

ROAD

GROVE MOOR
FARM

OPEN FIELDS

OPEN
FIELDS

GROVE

FIELDS

TRESWELL
WOOD

N
↑

NOT TO SCALE
WALK 7

ROAD

OPEN
FIELDS

WOOD

WOOD

WOOD

WOOD

WOOD

GROVE ROAD

WOOD

FIELDS

OPEN
FIELDS

WOOD

ROAD

LADYWELL
RISE

BOTTOM
WOODBECK
FARM

ROAD

ROAD

ROAD

OPEN
FIELDS

MINOR
ROAD

HEADON

START

P

OPEN
FIELDS

TO
UPTON

13

Walk 8: Clarborough Heights Walk
Walking Time: 2hrs 40mins   Distance: 12km 7.5miles
Start: GR 730839 Map No. 271

1. Park in housing estate near bend on A620 in Clarborough. Walk up hill
    for 200m to **PF** on right. Walk along back of long gardens 350m crossing
    4 stiles to minor road.
2. Ascend minor road look for **PF** sign at top going straight across bearing
    132°M from end of road. Go over hill to Red Flats Lane (track) following
    it round for 1.6km to meet Blue Stocking Lane (track).
3. Turn left for 50m then right at GR 753836 in direction of power station
    now ahead following arrows for Trent Valley Way. You are now on High
    House Road for 1.9km passing Maunhill Wood then under railway bridge.
4. 150m after bridge turn left walking to a railway crossing 300m further at
    GR 775839. Cross line through gate with care then walk 50m to a track
    junction. Turn right walking between 2 hedges.
5. Walk 200m, turn left on farm track to Field Farm. Just past farm
    buildings turn right across grass field bearing 344°M from corner to take
    you to a rusty 5 bar gate. Take general bearing here of 334°M passing to
    left of pylon in field. Look ahead for small post with white arrow to take
    you over footbridge.
6. Take general bearing 334°M from footbridge to walk for 720m to Muspit
    Lane (look for yellow arrow and stile). Turn left on lane for 1.5km then
    descend to Blue Stocking Lane.
7. Turn right walking NW direction on Blue Stocking Lane to emerge on
    A620 800m further on at Prospect House. Cross with case then cross stile
    at far side.
8. Bear left on general bearing 257°M rising to top of field. Go between
    some trees then cross a large field on a track to emerge on bend of
    Hangingside Lane (track) where you turn left.
9. Walk for 500m descending towards Hayton Village ahead. At 4-way
    byway/bridleway sign on the descent, turn left onto Lovers Walk (track),
    walking for 700m back to the start point. Turn right to descend hill to your
    parking place.

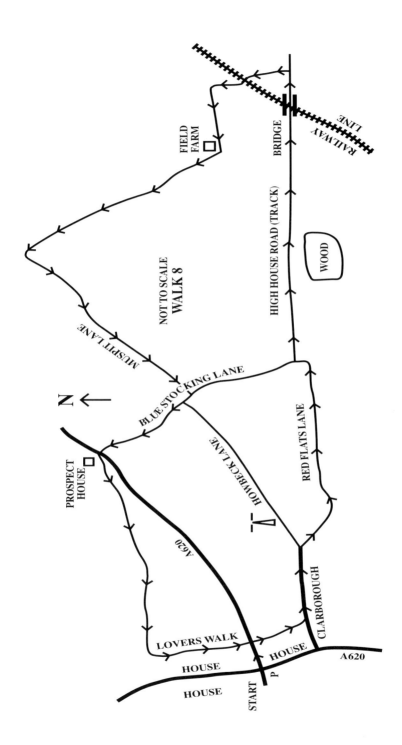

Walk 9: Barnby Moor / Canal Walk
Walk Time: 3hrs   Distance: 13.3km 8.3miles
Start: GR 664829 Map No. 279

1. Park in small **CP** at side of bridge north of Canal Cottages.
2. Walk under bridge on canal towpath passing lock. On reaching a brick bridge, bear right on an obvious track for 1.7km passing Low farm. You see A1 road ahead.
3. Walk to A1 then cross with extreme care on path provided. Sign states 'access to Bilby Farms only' also bridleway sign.
4. Continue on the long straight road to T-junction, turn left, passing Bilby Farm. The track goes between 2 houses then through double 5-bar gates.
5. Ascend slightly to a T-junction beside double 5-bar gates. Look for small blue arrow on post. Turn left on a narrow road following it round and passing Thievesdale Lane then crossing a disused airfield.
6. Pass a farm on left then through a 5-bar gate on the road between houses in Scofton Village. Continue on road ahead to Osberton Lock on the canal then turn left on to the towpath.
7. Stay on the towpath, passing Chequers Inn then continuing to the brick bridge where you originally turned off. Continue on the towpath back to the **CP**.

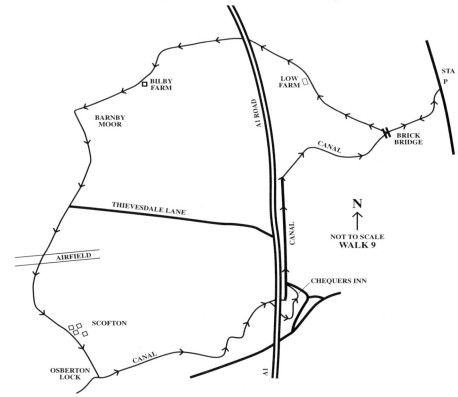

16